Visual Recipes

Visual Recipes

A Cookbook for Non-Readers

Tabitha Orth

APC

Autism Asperger Publishing Co.
P.O. Box 23173
Shawnee Mission, Kansas 66283-0173
www.asperger.net

APC

©2006 Autism Asperger Publishing Company
P.O. Box 23173
Shawnee Mission, KS 66283-0173
www.asperger.net

Publisher's Cataloging-in-Publication

Orth, Tabitha.

  Visual recipes : a cookbook for non-readers / Tabitha Orth. --
Shawnee Mission, Kan. : Autism Asperger Pub. Co., 2006.

    p. ; cm.
    ISBN-13: 978-1-931282-90-1
    ISBN-10: 1-931282-90-0
    LCCN 2006922939
    Previously published: New York, NY : DRL Books, c2000.
    Summary: This book contains step-by-step visual recipes to
help young children and individuals with autism and other
developmental disabilities prepare simple recipes.
    Includes index.

    1. Cookery for people with mental disabilities. 2. Cookery for
people with disabilities. 3. Cookery. I. Title.

TX652 .O78 2006
641.5/6–dc22   0605

Editor: John Eng

Cover Art: Ramon Gil

This book is designed in Helvetica Neue and Comic Sans.

Printed in the United States of America.

Dedicated to my son Matthew,
who teaches me patience daily
and humbles me with his
courage.

~~~

In loving memory of my father,
Edward Andrews.

Acknowledgments

I would like to extend my appreciation to the special students who tested these recipes, Matthew Orth, Michael James Hinchcliff, Simon Revitch and Michael Bailey. Their responses affirmed the detail that had to be included in the directions to accommodate the needs of a broad spectrum of people with developmental disabilities. My gratitude also extends to Nancy Hinchcliff, Hyanna Revitch, Cindy Bailey, and Zachary Carr for encouraging me in the belief that this book could help people find independence in the kitchen. Finally, to my models, Barbette Falk, Sharmane Bearcub and Tiana Schmitt, who quite literally lent me their hands.

I also extend my appreciation to the following companies for allowing their products to be pictured:

Aurora Foods, Inc.
> Duncan Hines Moist Deluxe White Cake

Bell-Carter Olive Company
> Lindsay Olives

Bradshaw International, Inc.
> Good Cook Measuring Cups and Spoons

Campbell Soup Company
> Franco-American Spaghetti

Church and Dwight Co. Inc.
> Arm and Hammer Baking Soda

"© 2000 The Coca-Cola Company. Minute Maid® is a registered trademark of The Coca-Cola Company."
> Minute Maid® Frozen Orange Juice

Continental Mills, Inc.
Bakery Chef, Inc.
> Krusteaz Mini-Pancakes

"© 1997 Del Monte Foods. Used with Permission."
> Del Monte Traditional Spaghetti Sauce

Diamond of California
> Diamond Walnuts

Eagle Family Food, Inc.
> ReaLemon

Table of Contents

Introduction

I have always enjoyed spending time in the kitchen creating meals for my friends and family. Since it doesn't take me long to fix a meal or special dessert, I felt instant gratification in seeing the results of my work as well as the pleasure of watching others enjoy my efforts. I also have fond memories of spending time in my mother's kitchen growing up, either watching her work or helping her in some way. I wanted to pass this on to my son. This was one mother-child experience I didn't want to miss out on, but I needed to think carefully about how I would start our cooking adventures together, since my son has autism and it severely affects his life.

Learning basic skills in the kitchen was an important goal to set for my son. Helping him reach his potential and become as independent in life as he possibly can be has been my mantra, as it is for all parents who have a child with a developmental disability. Cooking and creating a meal or snack independently would also give him a sense of pride and personal accomplishment, I figured. It was a skill that he could learn to be confident in. The question was what would be the most successful way to teach him. This book is my answer to that question.

UNDERSTANDING YOUR COOKING STUDENT'S LEARNING STYLE

This book was written and designed to address the needs of children between the ages of 3 and 10 years old, as well as individuals with autism and other developmental disabilities, regardless of their age. Individuals who do not read (the young children) as well as others who are very visually oriented (many individuals with developmental disorders) depend heavily on the visual information they receive to understand the world around them.

Since it is difficult for a young child to hold on to long pieces of verbal instruction, classrooms around the country utilize a variety of visual signs, labels and picture directions to present information clearly and concretely. In beginning grade levels, therefore, signs for the music area, play area, reading area, arts and crafts areas, etc., are boldly expressed in colorful, eye-catching pictures with words to define a classroom's perimeters and expectations. As students progress through school, the visual information is not faded, but modified as students' skills improve. Charts, graphs, sign-in sheets, maps, and written instructions, sometimes accompanied by examples or visual symbols, are some of the familiar tools used in a student's school day.

Why is it that we depend on visual information so intensely in our daily lives? It is because visual information is not transient! We can refer to a visual direction time and time again to reassure ourselves that we are on the right track. On the other hand, when we receive information verbally, we have to work harder. We have to take the information in, understand it, and organize it so we can react and respond promptly and correctly. This type of processing is difficult for young children and is a core deficit for people with autism and other developmental disabilities. However, the greater part of our population also depends on visual information to help us function successfully and more effortlessly throughout our day. This is why, as a society, we have incorporated a wide array of visual communication tools and strategies.

Let's look at what might be a typical morning for a working professional. She checks her daily planner or calendar for events scheduled for the day. She notices that a meeting is scheduled with a vendor at an unfamiliar location. Following a map and referring to the address on the vendor's business card, she arrives at the office building and parks in a numbered parking spot in a color-coded parking structure. After getting out of the car, she follows the arrow signs that lead to the entrance of the building. There she locates the office directory to confirm the correct floor where the meeting is to take place. Glancing at the clock and referring to the appointment card, she sees that she is right on time, so she proceeds toward the designated room. Upon arriving at the meeting, she signs in, puts on her name tag and accepts a copy of the agenda.

The visual supports that the average person uses throughout a day are substantial. We rely on these tools and strategies to avoid stress and confusion. Considering how much we rely on visual tools to support our unimpaired memories, cognitive functioning, organizational and processing abilities, let's look at which level of support a person with a developmental disability need to be successful.

People with autism are visual learners as are most people with developmental disabilities. They actually think in pictures. Whereas most of us have thoughts and ideas going through our minds, they see the picture by drawing from their experiences as if to bring up the right video or CD ROM image in their memory banks. This strength is finely tuned, and one they depend upon for accurately receiving, processing, understanding and expressing information. Since persons with autism spectrum disorders also have difficulty organizing and sequencing information, and are often challenged with a delay in their processing, the best way to achieve success with such students is to teach utilizing their strengths while supporting their deficits.

About *Visual Recipes*

Common sense tells us that when we teach someone something new, we want to approach the lesson using all his strengths and skills. *Visual Recipes* does just that.

Each aspect of the design and formatting of *Visual Recipes* is supporting a deficit while at the same time utilizing a strength. Understanding the intent behind the design helps you to better understand the needs of the person you will be working with. First, notice that the directions move from left to right on each page, working from the top of the page downward. This builds on our natural tendency to move our eyes from left to right. It is how we learn to scan and read, and usually how we begin working on a task. When you wash a window, do you tend to start at the upper-left corner? You most likely do, and this is because it is a comfortable strategy. As you will also note, each step in a recipe is framed, which helps the person stay organized, giving him the visual information he needs. Also, using only three framed steps across a page enables the person to find his place more easily, supporting any problems he might have sequencing information. Pictures have been edited to give clear and concrete information. Safety is highlighted by calling attention to the use of oven mitts and turning off stove and oven dials to support a student who has difficulty with judgment. Although the visuals are self-explanatory, short, concrete written directions accompany each step. The text was carefully chosen and repeated in each similar step throughout the book to provide opportunities for developing sight reading skills or reinforcing present sight reading skills across materials. Lastly, color and number matching has been embedded in the directions to support the non-reader and the student who lacks the mathematical skills of measuring fractions. The breakdown of each recipe, which includes many steps that might seem unnecessary to some, creates a unique format that allows a student to become independent in the kitchen with greater confidence and ease.

TIPS AND TRICKS

Presentation

Many people with autism spectrum disorders and other developmental disabilities need visual supports to go with picture directions. Cooking offers a built-in, direct object visual system. That system consists of the ingredients and utensils needed for the recipe. When all the materials are made available to your student, you will instantly be able to assess if the student is capable of organizing the cooking supplies that are gathered. Does he follow the visual recipe, selecting the right ingredients, or does he appear to need additional help? If your student is struggling with a deficit in organizational skills and has trouble finding the next object needed, for example, line the ingredients up from left to right in the order that they will be used in the recipe. The student will match the picture to the object more easily since he is no longer confronted with having to work his way through clutter.

Note: For students who do not have problems with generalization, a product other than the one pictured may be substituted. These students would be able to follow the visual directions and object system successfully.

Motor Planning Obstacles

Be aware of any motor planning issues a student has and, whenever possible, adjust the materials used to add support. For example, a student who has trouble opening a jar might do better with a squeeze bottle. Many of the ingredients that are used in this book are now marketed in squeeze bottles such as mayonnaise, margarine, pizza sauce, jellies/jams, and peanut butter. An electric can opener might be a better option than a manual one. The timer you choose should be easily read and have a sound that does not aggravate any auditory hypersensitivities. Consider your student's needs when deciding on a push button timer versus a turn dial timer. Spend time in the cooking section of stores to get ideas for adaptive equipment that could benefit your student. Years ago I came across a battery-operated flour sifter and thought all my wishes had come true!

Beyond the Kitchen

To add greater scope to your teaching, use the contents of the directions in *Visual Recipes* to teach functional math and beginning reading skills. Build a sight reading program based on the text used in the recipes, or introduce fractions by practicing measuring ingredients in a one-on-one teaching time. These skills can be generalized later.

COLOR CODING YOUR KITCHEN

Color highlights important information. For individuals who have difficulty matching numbers to numbers or words to words, relying on color matching skills will lead them to greater independence in the kitchen. The easiest way to color code is to use color-coded sticker dots (found in office supply stores) or electrical tape. Both are commonly packaged in multicolor variety packs with all four primary colors. If you want to get fancy, you can purchase replacement stove and oven dials to match the recipes or blank ones to create color wheel dials. You can even buy color-coded measuring cups and spoons that match the color coding used in this book (Good Cook, a product of Bradshaw International).

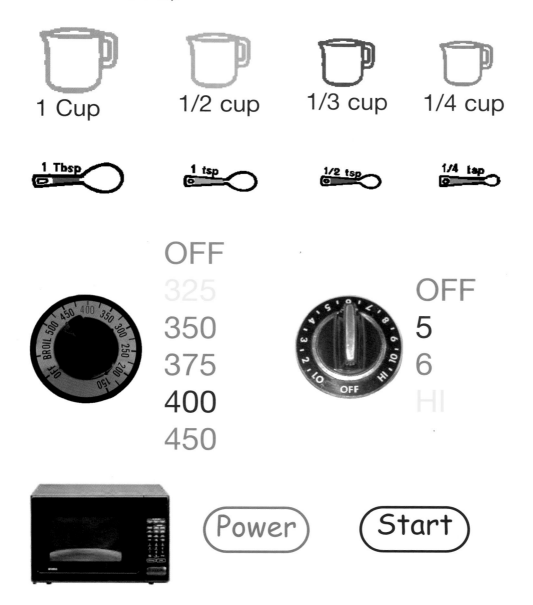

Making Oatmeal

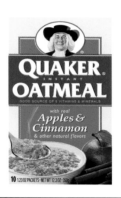

Cut open package.

Empty package into bowl.

Put paper in trash.

Heat water.

Measure 1/2 cup hot water.

Pour hot water into bowl.

Stir.

Enjoy.

Scrambled eggs 	Get 2 eggs.	Crack egg into bowl. 
Crack second egg. 	Scramble eggs with fork. 	Measure 1 Tablespoon butter. 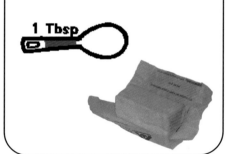
Put butter in pan. 	Turn stove dial to '5'. 	When butter melts, 

Pour in
egg mixture.

Use a
spatula

to push
eggs around
in pan.

Push eggs
with spatula
to cook.

Push eggs
with spatula
to cook.

Push eggs
with spatula
to cook.

Turn stove
dial to 'Off'.

Put eggs
on plate.

Enjoy.

Golden Patties	Making Golden patties.	Turn oven on to BAKE 450.

Put on baking sheet.	Put on oven mitts.	Put in oven.
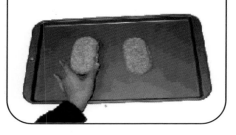		
Close oven door.	Take off oven mitts.	Set timer for 15 minutes.

Turn off beeping timer.	Put on oven mitts.	Take out of oven.
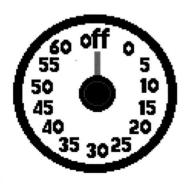		
Cool on rack.	Close oven door.	Take off oven mitts.
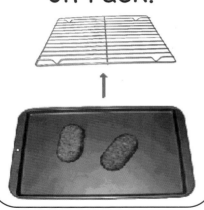		
Turn oven dial to 'Off'.	Put on plate.	Enjoy.

Toasted Bagel with Cream Cheese. 	Cut bagel in half. 	Put bagels in toaster. 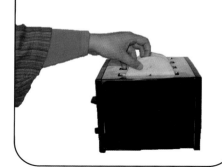
Push down. 	Bagels pop up when toasted. 	Put bagels on plate. 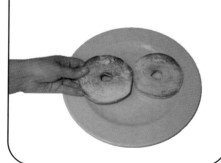
Get cream cheese. 	Scoop with knife. 	Spread on bagel. 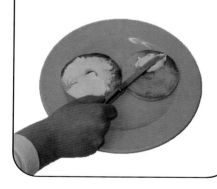

Enjoy.

Pancakes and Sausage

Get

Put pancakes on plate.

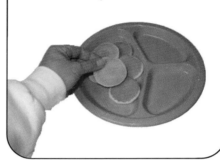

Put sausage on plate.

Get syrup.

Pour syrup on pancakes.

Put in microwave.

Close door.

Power

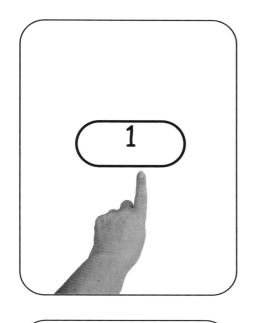

1

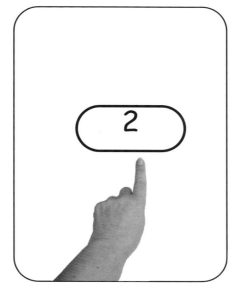

2

0

Start

Take out
of microwave.

Enjoy.

Toast 	Put bread in toaster. 	Push down on handle.
Toast pops up when ready. 	Put toast on a plate. 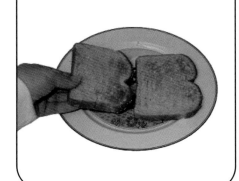	Cut some butter. 
Spread butter on toast. 	Enjoy. 	

English Muffins	Put muffins in toaster.	Push down to toast.

Muffins will pop up when ready.	Take out toasted muffins.	Put on plate.

Cut some butter.	Spread butter on muffin.	Enjoy.
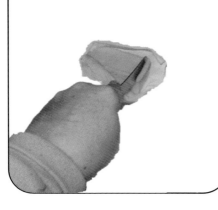	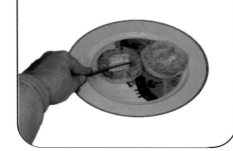	

Bologna Sandwich	Get 2 slices of bread.	Open mayonnaise.

Spread mayonnaise.	Spread mayonnaise.	Get bologna.

Put 2 pieces of bologna on bread.	Put bread on top.	Cut in half.
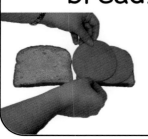		

Put on plate.

Enjoy.

Peanut Butter & Jelly Sandwich 	Get 2 slices of bread. 	Open peanut butter. 
Spread peanut butter. 	Put lid back on. 	Open jelly. 
Spread jelly on bread. 	Put lid back on jelly. 	Put together 

to make a
sandwich.

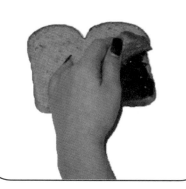

Cut
sandwich.

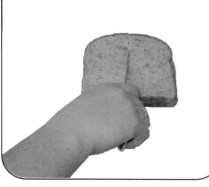

Put on
plate.

Enjoy.

Tuna Fish Sandwich	Get out a can of tuna.	Open can. Push down on handle.
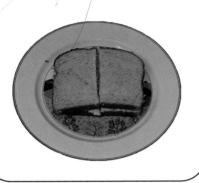		
Lift up to remove can.	Drain water from tuna can.	Drain water from tuna can.

Take off lid.	Put tuna in a bowl.	Flake tuna with a fork.

Get mayonnaise.	Measure 2 tablespoons mayonnaise.	Put mayonnaise in bowl.

Mix tuna with a fork.	Add 3 shakes of pepper.	Stir.

Spread mayonnaise.	Spread tuna.	Put bread on top.

Put on plate and cut.	Enjoy.
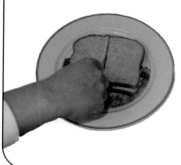	

Grilled Cheese Sandwich 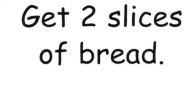	Get 2 slices of bread. 	Put bread in toaster. 
Push down on handle to toast. 	Bread pops up when toasted. 	Take out toast. 
Get 2 slices of cheese. 	Take off plastic wrap. 	Put cheese on toast. 

Put cheese on toast.

Put bread on top.

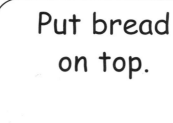

Put on plate.

Put in microwave.

Close door.

Power

2

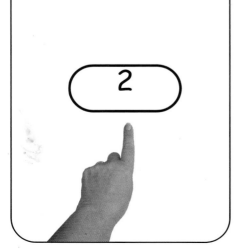

5

Start

Take out
of microwave.

The cheese
will be melted.

Cut in half.

Enjoy.

Pizza 	Measure 1/4 cup flour. 	Pour flour. 
Spread out flour. 	Coat flour in dough. 	Grease pan. 
Put dough on pan. 	Roll out dough. 	Roll out dough. 

Get spaghetti sauce.	Open can. Push down.	Lift. Remove can and lid.

Pour on sauce.	Spread sauce.	Grate cheese.
	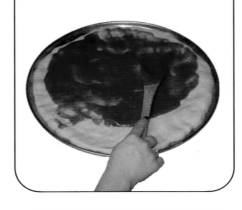	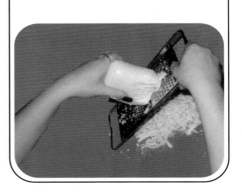
Put grated cheese in bowl.	Sprinkle cheese on pizza.	Get pepperoni.

Put on pepperoni.

Get can of olives.

Open olives.

Lift.
Remove can and lid.

Drain olives.

Put olives on pizza.

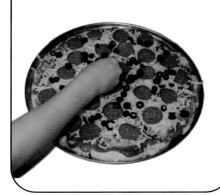

Turn oven on to BAKE 350.

Put on oven mitts.

Put in oven.

Take off oven mitts. 	Set timer for 30 minutes. 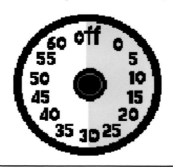	Turn off beeping timer. 
Put on oven mitts. 	Take pizza out of oven. 	Close oven door. 
Turn oven dial to 'Off'. 	Cut pizza. 	Put slice on plate. Enjoy. 

Heating a Slice of Pizza

Get a slice of pizza.	Put on plate.

Put in microwave.	Close door.	Power

4	0	Start
	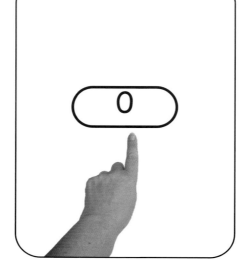	

Take out of microwave.

Enjoy.

Hot dog on a bun	Get a hot dog.	Put on plate.

Put in microwave.	Close door.	
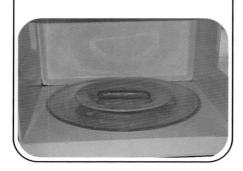		Power 

2 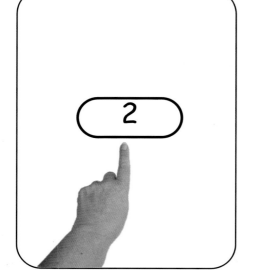	5 	Start 

44

Take out
of microwave.

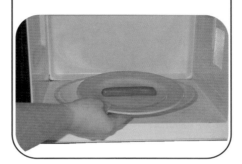

Put hot dog
on a bun.

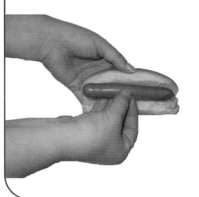

Put on a
plate.

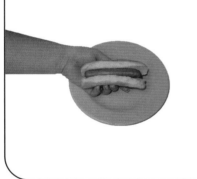

Enjoy your
hot dog.

Corn dog 	Get a corn dog. 	Put it on a plate. 
Put in microwave. 	Close door. 	Power 
5 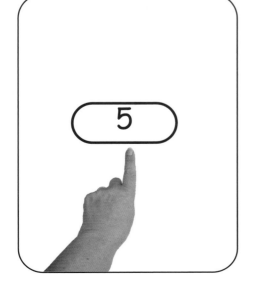	0 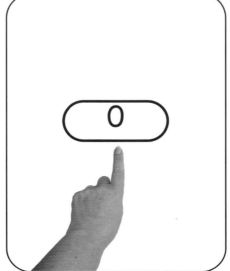	Start 

Take out of microwave.

Enjoy.

Ravioli 	Open can. Push. 	Lift up. Remove lid. 
Pour into pot. 	Put lid in trash. 	Turn stove dial to '6'. 
Stir. 	When ravioli starts to bubble. 	Turn stove dial to Off. 

Pour ravioli into bowl.

Enjoy.

Spaghetti	Open can. Push down.	Lift up. Remove lid.

Put lid in the trash.	Pour spaghetti into pot.	Turn stove on to '6'.

Stir.	When it starts to bubble,	Turn stove dial to Off.

Pour hot spaghetti into bowl.

Enjoy.

Baked Chicken 	**Get out chicken.** 	**Wash Chicken.** 
Turn oven to Bake 400. 	**Cut open seasoning packet.** 	**Pour onto plate.** 
Coat chicken with seasoning. 	**Turn over. Coat the other side.** 	**Get out a baking sheet.** 

Put chicken on baking sheet.	Put on oven mitts.	Put in oven.

Set timer for 20 minutes.	Take off oven mitts.	Turn off beeping timer.

Put on oven mitts.	Take chicken out of oven.	Cool on rack.
		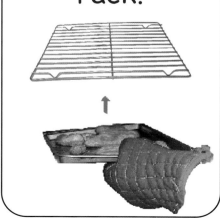

Cool.

Turn oven to 'Off'.

Serve.

Minute Rice	Measure 2 cups of water.	Pour water into pot.

Turn stove dial to 'Hi'.	Get out butter.	Cut a thick slice of butter.

Add butter to boiling water.	Measure 2 cups rice.	Pour in rice.
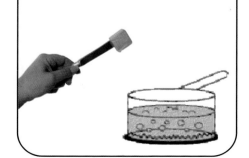		

Turn stove dial to 'Off'.	Put lid on pot.	Put on an oven mitt.

Remove pot from stove.	Take off oven mitt.	Set timer for 5 minutes.

Turn off beeping timer.	Get serving spoon.	Serve.

Tater Tots	Turn oven on to BAKE 450.	Get baking sheet.

Put on baking sheet.	Put on oven mitts.	Put in oven.

Close oven door.	Take off oven mitts.	Set timer for 15 minutes.

Turn off beeping timer.	Put on oven mitts.	Take out of oven.

Turn oven dial to 'Off'.	Cool on rack.	Put on plate.
	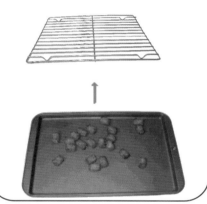	
Enjoy.		

Broccoli	Cut broccoli stalks.	Wash broccoli.
	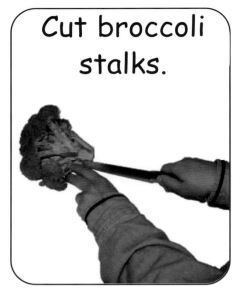	
Put broccoli in pot. Add water.	Put on stove.	Turn stove dial to 'Hi'.

Set timer for 5 minutes.	Cook broccoli.	Turn off beeping timer.

Turn stove dial to 'Off'.

Remove from heat.

Strain.

Pour into bowl.

Enjoy.

Carrots 	Wash carrots. 	Get out peeler. 
Peel carrots. 	Cut off end of carrot. 	Cut off end of carrot. 
Slice. 	Fill pot with water. 	Put carrots in pot. 

Put pot on stove.

Turn stove dial to 'Hi'.

When water boils,

turn stove dial to '5'.

Set timer for 5 minutes.

Turn off beeping timer.

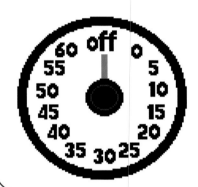

Turn stove dial to 'Off'.

Drain water.

Pour into bowl.

Get out butter.

Add some butter to carrots.

Enjoy.

French Fries	Get out french fries.	Get out baking sheet.

Turn oven on to BAKE 450.	Cut open bag.	Pour french fries onto baking sheet.

Put on oven mitts.	Put in oven.	Take off oven mitts.
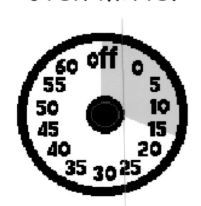		

Set timer for 15 minutes.	Turn off beeping timer.	Put on oven mitts.

Take out of oven.	Take off oven mitts.	Turn oven dial to 'Off'.

Get spatula.	Scoop up french fries.	Put on plate.

Popcorn

Get a 3 OZ package of popcorn.

Put in microwave.

Close door.

Power

2

2

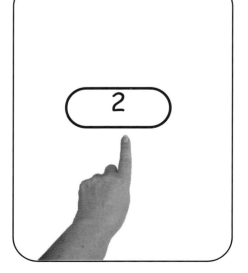

0

Start

Take out
of microwave.

Open bag.
Be careful.
It is hot.

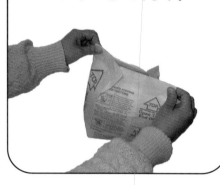

Pour.

Enjoy.

Chocolate Pudding	Get a bowl.	Measure 2 cups milk.

Pour into bowl.	Cut open pudding mix.	Pour in mix.

Set timer for 2 minutes.	Beat.	Turn off beeping timer.
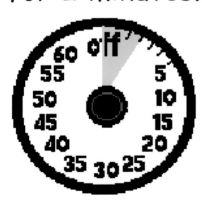		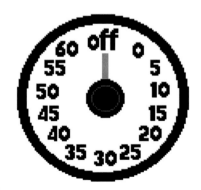

Pour into 4 bowls. 	Put in refrigerator. 	Close door. 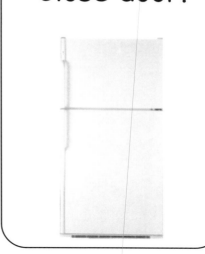
Set timer for 5 minutes. 	When timer beeps, 	Take out of refrigerator. 
Enjoy. 		

Celery and Peanut Butter	Wash celery. 	Cut off each end.
Cut off end. 	Cut celery in half. 	Get peanut butter. 
Open. 	Spread peanut butter on celery. 	Enjoy. 

Sliced Apple

Wash apple.

Turn off faucet.

Put slicer on top of apple.

Push down.

Push!

Put in bowl.

Brownies

Turn oven on to BAKE 350.

Get Crisco.

Get 9 x 13 baking pan.

Grease pan.

Cut open bag of mix.

Pour mix into bowl.

Measure 1/4 cup water.

Add water.

Get 2 eggs. Crack open.	Put into bowl.	Measure 1/2 cup vegetable oil.
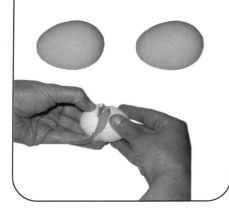		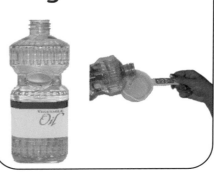
Mix well.	Get a rubber spatula.	Pour batter into pan.

Spread evenly.	Put on oven mitts.	Put in oven.

Take off oven mitts.	Set timer for 30 minutes.	Turn off beeping timer.
	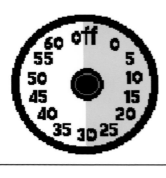	
Put on oven mitts.	Take out brownies.	Put on rack to cool.

Take off oven mitts.	Turn oven dial to 'Off'.	Insert toothpick to see if done.

Cut and serve.

Cupcakes 	Turn oven on to BAKE 325. 	Cut open bag of mix. 
Pour mix into bowl. 	Add 2 tablespoons vegetable oil. 	Get 3 eggs. 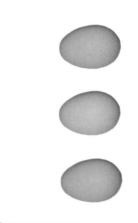
Crack eggs open. Put into bowl. 	Add 1 + 1/3 cups water. 	Beat well. 

Get a 9" x 5" x 3" loaf pan.	Get Crisco.	Grease loaf pan.

Pour batter into pan.	**Put on oven mitts.**	**Put in oven.**
		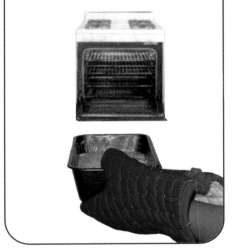
Take off oven mitts.	**Set timer for 48 minutes.**	**Turn off beeping timer.**
	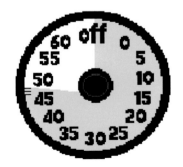	

Put on oven mitts.	Take out of oven.	Close oven door.

Put on rack to cool.	Take off oven mitts.	Turn oven dial to 'Off'.
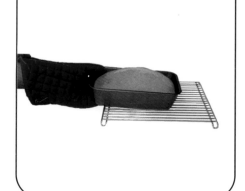		
Cut when cooled.	Serve.	Enjoy.

Chocolate Chip Cookies 	Get out a large bowl. 	Add 1 bar soft butter. 
Measure 1 cup butter flavored Crisco. 	Add to bowl. 	Measure 1/2 cup + 1/4 cup sugar. 
Add to bowl. 	Mix well. 	Get 2 eggs.

Crack egg into bowl.	Mix well.	Add 2 teaspoons vanilla.

Add 1 teaspoon salt.	Add 1 teaspoon baking soda.	Add 2 + 1/4 cups flour.

Mix well.	Add 1 bag chocolate chips.	Add 1 cup walnuts.

Mix well.

Turn oven on to BAKE 375.

Get Crisco.

Grease cookie sheet.

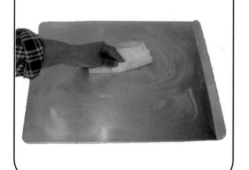

Get a cookie scooper.

Scoop up dough.

Scoop dough onto cookie sheet.

Put on oven mitts.

Put cookies in oven.

Close oven door.	Take off oven mitts.	Set timer for 10 minutes.

Turn off beeping timer.	Put on oven mitts.	Take out the cookies.

Put on cooling rack.	Take off oven mitts.	Remove and cool.

Turn oven
dial to 'Off'.

Enjoy.

Banana Muffins	Turn oven on to BAKE 350.	Measure 2/3 cups sugar.

Add 6 tablespoons soft butter.	Add 1 teaspoon lemon juice.	Mix well.

Get 3 bananas and peal.	Cut bananas in slices.	Put banana in bowl.

Beat in bananas.	Get 2 eggs. Crack open.	Put into bowl.

Beat well.	Measure 1 cup chopped walnuts.	Add to bowl.

Mix in nuts.	Add 1/4 teaspoon salt.	Add 3/4 teaspoons baking powder.

Add 1 teaspoon baking soda. 	Add 1 and 1/3 cups flour. 	Mix well. 
Put paper liners in pan. 	Spoon in batter until 3/4 full. 	Put on oven mitts. 
Put in oven. 	Close oven door. 	Take off oven mitts. 

Set timer for 20 minutes.	Turn off beeping timer.	Put on oven mitts.

Take out of oven.	Put on cooling rack.	Take off oven mitts.

Turn oven dial to 'Off'.	Let muffins cool.	Enjoy.

Swiss Miss	Open Swiss Miss.	Measure 1 Teaspoon.

Put in mug.	Measure 1 teaspoon.	Put in mug.

Heat water.	Pour water.	Stir.

Put lid on.

Enjoy.

Orange Juice 	Get. 	Pull tab to open. 
Pour orange juice into pitcher. 	Fill can with water. 	Pour into pitcher. 
Fill can with water. 	Pour into pitcher. 	Fill can with water. 

Pour into pitcher.	Stir.	Pour juice.

Enjoy.

Ice Tea	Get ice tea mix.	Open.

Measure 1 Tablespoon of mix.	Pour into tall glass.	Measure 1 Tablespoon of mix.

Pour into glass.	Put lid on.	Add water.

Add ice cubes.	Stir.	Enjoy.

Index

Read AAPC's Entire Practical Solutions Series

Asperger Syndrome and Difficult Moments: Practical Solutions for Tantrums, Rage, and Meltdowns – *Revised and Expanded Edition*
Brenda Smith Myles and Jack Southwick

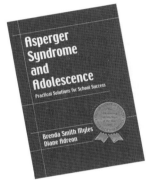

Asperger Syndrome and Adolescence: Practical Solutions for School Success
Brenda Smith Myles and Diane Adreon

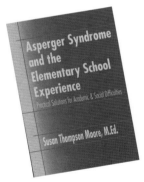

Asperger Syndrome and the Elementary School Experience: Practical Solutions for Academic & Social Difficulties
Susan Thompson Moore

Asperger Syndrome and Sensory Issues: Practical Solutions for Making Sense of the World
Brenda Smith Myles, Katherine Tapscott Cook, Nancy E. Miller, Louann Rinner, and
Lisa A. Robbins

Finding Our Way: Practical Solutions for Creating a Supportive Home and Community for the Asperger Syndrome Family
Kristi Sakai; foreword by Brenda Smith Myles

The Hidden Curriculum: Practical Solutions for Understanding Unstated Rules in Social Situations
Brenda Smith Myles, Melissa L. Trautman, and Ronda L. Schelvan; foreword by Michelle Garcia Winner

Perfect Targets: Asperger Syndrome and Bullying; Practical Solutions for Surviving the Social World
Rebekah Heinrichs

Practical Solutions to Everyday Challenges for Children with Asperger Syndrome
Haley Morgan Myles

To order, go to: www.asperger.net

AAPC

Autism Asperger Publishing Co.
P.O. Box 23173
Shawnee Mission, Kansas 66283-0173
www.asperger.net